# Making Adjustments

*Meditations on Learning with Children*

## Misa Okayama

edited by Ann Pelo
and Margie Carter

**E**

Exchange
Press

PRAISE FOR *MAKING ADJUSTMENTS*

Misa's meditations on her interactions with and her relationship to five-year-old Tsuki are an invitation to each of us to slow down, to be present and to discover infinite possibility in our lives as educators and as students of life. For all who desire to bring their whole selves to the classroom, Misa shares how it can be done, bringing a cultural and intimately personal lens to the daily practice of teaching. One can taste the richness that comes when one deeply understands that the reference to that magical teaching moment is not only for the child but for all of us.

**Lisa Lee,** *Early Childhood Educator*

This slim little book can be read in one sitting, but don't! Take the time to read it slowly and mindfully, savoring the deeper meaning behind the simple story of a child building a motorcycle. Pause and think about the meditative and reflective questions at the end of each chapter. Then when you've read the whole book, go back and read it again. You'll find hidden gems that you missed the first time around.

**Barbara Yasui,** *Retired Educator*
*and Racial Equity Trainer*

ISBN 978-0-942702-80-4

eISBN 978-0-942702-81-1

Printed in the United States.

Book Design: Stacy Hawthorne and Scott Bilstad

Editors: Ann Pelo and Margie Carter

Managing Editor: Erin Glenn

Photographs provided by Misa Okayama.

For more information about other Exchange Press publications and resources for directors and teachers, contact:

Exchange Press

7700 A Street

Lincoln, NE 68510

(800) 221-2864 • ExchangePress.com

## A Call to Reimagine Our Work

The stories in the *Reimagining Our Work* (ROW) collection are anchored in the conviction that another world is possible for early childhood education—a world characterized by open-hearted and attentive collaborations between children and educators, in shared exploration of engaging ideas. This collection helps us begin to imagine that world, as we reimagine our work, moving beyond the joyless land of prescribed curricula with its corresponding outcomes and assessments, into the unpredictable, green-growing terrain of lively curiosity and rigorous critical thought.

Too often in our field, the discourse about educators reflects a diminished and disrespectful view of their capabilities for challenging, rigorous, generative thought. "Keep things simple and easily digestible," is a common caution. "Teachers want strategies that they can put immediately to use in their classrooms. Don't offer too much theory, too much complexity."

We disagree. **Strongly.** We believe that educators hunger for deeper meaning in their work. We believe that educators long to be challenged into their biggest, deepest, most startling thinking and questioning. We believe that educators are ready to have their hearts cracked open and their imaginations ignited. We believe that educators are eager to explore how theory looks in everyday practice and how practice can inform theory. These convictions are at the heart of this collection of stories.

In these stories, children and educators take up ideas of substance, pursuing questions in ways that are unscripted and original. They braid fluid imagination and expansive awareness into their collaborative inquiry. The children in these stories aren't "gifted" or privileged—except by the gift and privilege of their educators' potent regard for their capability, and their concomitant willingness to bring their best minds and hearts to the table.

Which is just what we see the educators do in these stories. We hear educators reflect—in their unique voices and contexts—on their evolving understandings of children's capacities, and their roles as educators, and the meaning and practice of teaching and learning. The educators in these stories hold assumptions and visions different from the dominant paradigm in our field, and we have much to learn from them.

With the ROW collection, we hope to advance the conversation among early childhood educators, administrators, community college and university educators, policy makers and funders about the nature and practice of early education—a conversation which we also engage in the foundational book for this collection,

*From Teaching to Thinking: A Pedagogy for Reimagining Our Work*. As you read, we hope that you are challenged, exhilarated, unsettled, and rejuvenated. We hope that you find kinship in these stories. We hope that the stories in this collection carry your thinking far beyond curriculum ideas, and help you reimagine your work. May these stories sustain you as you stand strong with the children in your care. Resist the limitations of standardized curriculum, and claim, instead, the exhilaration of creating a new world, together with children.

—*Ann Pelo* and *Margie Carter*
   Editors of the *Reimagining Our Work* (ROW) Collection

   Authors of *From Teaching to Thinking: A Pedagogy for Reimagining Our Work*

For more information on the
ROW collection and upcoming titles
please visit ExchangePress.com/ROW

# Contents

# Foreword

Philosopher and motorcycle mechanic Matthew Crawford[1] offers a potent glimpse into our human psyches in his book *The World Beyond Your Head.* He writes: "Attention is the thing that is most one's own: in the normal course of things, we choose what to pay attention to, and in a very real sense this determines what is real for us; what is actually present to our consciousness."

Rooted inside this bold declaration is an essential question: What do you want to be real for you?

What will you pay attention to, as a human being and as an educator? Where will you focus your gaze? What do you want to be real for you?

Misa Sensei 先生 teaches us about attention in her quiet, remarkable book, *Making Adjustments: Meditations on Learning with Children.* Misa keeps her gaze on a moment she shares with five-year-old Tsuki, and lets that moment captivate her attention. Her commitment of attention opens Misa into a kaleidoscope of ways that she can understand her exchange

---

1) Matthew Crawford, *The World Beyond Your Head: On Becoming an Individual in an Age of Distraction.* (New York: Farrar, Straus and Giroux, 2015)

with Tsuki. She meditates on Japanese proverbs and cultural values, Maori wisdom, and her school's legacy of activism.

This is the art of attention, illuminated by the practice of meditation.

**Meditation:** a way of listening. The practice of training our attention and awareness, which braids focus together with an attitude of openness and curiosity. There are many types of meditation, and the through-line that connects them is this: we quiet ourselves and turn our attention to one thing—our breath, or gratitude, or loving-kindness—or a moment we've shared with a child.

And when our attention wanders, we gently call it back.

We remind ourselves what we want to be real for us in the days that we share with children.

Matthew Crawford cautions us that "appropriations of our attention are ... an especially intimate matter." Intimate, because what we give our attention to becomes real for us. Many things vie for our attention as educators: health and safety mandates and the stresses that come with them;

staffing crunches that leave us stretched and weary; expectations that every moment be seized to teach academic skills with curriculum scripts that define the content of children's days; stifling pressures to assess and document children's learning. When these concerns steal our attention away from what we most value and cherish, our work is to call our attention back to what we want to make real, back to where we want to dedicate our consciousness. Our work is to call our attention back to the children.

Misa writes about this decision to focus our attention on children in the context of their "human right to be seen."

"Being fully present to each child, in the here and now, is the most powerful thing we can do to help the children learn to deeply know themselves," writes Misa. "This is our great responsibility." When we commit our attention to children in this way, "we enrich our own souls, too. It lifts us out of the confined roles of educators, and asks us to see another person from the perspective of a fellow human being. We encounter the many colorful ways that people can be, rather than relating to children through a narrow lens of 'learning goals' or 'school readiness.' And this nurtures our growth, too."

This isn't easy, for sure. Being present to each child in the here and now requires a disciplined mind and committed heart, a vigilant alertness to distractions, just as meditation does. It asks us to disrupt our habit of jumping from one thought to another—what some meditation practitioners call "monkey mind." As educators, we experience "monkey mind" when we see a group of children building an elaborate playscape in the block area, with stuffed animals and dishes and fabric, and our thinking jumps past the integrity of the children's play to fret about clean-up, as we check the clock to see how close we are to lunchtime. We experience monkey mind when we absent-mindedly watch a baby reaching for the rainbows cast by the prism in the window while we do a mental inventory of the diaper supply, wonder if the bleach water at the diaper table is good for another hour, and consider where we'll get take-out on our lunch break. Pressures to efficiently use every minute for teaching or assessment feed our monkey minds.

Misa's book is an invitation to quiet our minds so that we can give our steady attention to the children with whom we spend our days. The ancient meaning of the word "meditation" asks us to "take appropriate measures[2]." And the Old Latin verb "to

---

2) Etymonline: Online Etymology Dictionary.

meditate" means "to plan, devise, practice, rehearse, study." When we slow down to think and wonder about the resonances in children's play, we are taking appropriate measures to strengthen our capacity for thoughtful and deliberate study. We practice the art of attention.

All of this matters because our energy, and our action, goes where our attention goes. We must be deliberate about giving our attention to the children with whom we spend our days, so that we can undertake "our great responsibility" as educators: being present to each child, in the here and now, honoring their human right to be seen, to be known. We pay attention in order to become more skilled at paying attention; our goal in this circular practice is to be of service to children, as they "learn to deeply know themselves." And self-knowledge is central to our capacity to live a vibrant life, with intention and conviction, empathy and generosity.

Meditation teacher Sharon Salzberg[3] writes: "One of my meditation teachers said that the most important moment in your meditation practice is the moment you sit down to

---

3) Sharon Salzberg, *Real Happiness: The Power of Meditation.* (New York: Workman Publishing, 2011)

do it. Because right then you're saying to yourself that you believe in change, you believe in caring for yourself, and you're making it real. You're not just holding some value like mindfulness or compassion in the abstract, but really making it real."

As you sit down with Misa's book, you have an opportunity to reconnect with what you want to pay attention to—with what you want to be real for you—as a human being and as an educator. With Misa, you can commit yourself to being present to children, and to yourself. You are committing your attention to learning with children, and, so, making that learning real. Read this book slowly, in the spirit of meditation, breath by breath. The riches that Misa offers—the metaphors and proverbs that open into insight and understanding—deserve to be savored.

Savoring requires time. And savoring offers deep nourishment.

Take time to exhale between each chapter rather than inhaling the whole book at once. Misa offers soul-deep questions for you to contemplate after each chapter—questions about who you long to be as an educator and as a human being, questions about how you can align your work with your intention to nurture children's humanity and your own. Take time with these questions. Quiet yourself and give your full attention to these invitations for contemplation.

The Kanji word for meditation or contemplation is *jyukkou*, 熟考. Misa offers this insight into the meanings of this word:

> The first character, 熟 has meanings around "ripen" or "mature." The second character, 考 is the character for "thinking." So the implication could be something like "to ripen your thoughts," or maybe even "the ripening *process* of your thoughts."

> I also recognize that the bottom part of this character, "熟," with the four lines, symbolizes fire. (For example, the character, 煮 is boiling, 蒸 is steaming, 熱 is heat.)

> Having said that, 熟考—contemplating and thinking about something deeply—is, in a way, like the slow-cooking process.

Misa's book of meditations invites us to slow our pace. Her questions for contemplation carry us into quiet space in which we can linger with our thoughts, allowing them to ripen in the warmth of our steady attention. And in that warm quiet, where we are present to ourselves, we find the gifts of new understandings and insights about what we value most dearly in our days with children, and in our lives.

**—Ann Pelo and Margie Carter**

Editors of the *Reimagining Our Work* (ROW) Collection

Authors of *From Teaching to Thinking: A Pedagogy for Reimagining Our Work*

# An
# Invitation

A child's play unfolds in many layers, with multiple stories to explore, multiple meanings and questions. Play is not just about what a child is learning, but what they're teaching us adults. A child's play can remind us of the depth of the world we live in.

There is not just one way to think about a moment with a child. When we linger with the play and listen to its many resonances, a kaleidoscope of possible understandings reveals itself. We can meditate on those complex patterns and startling illuminations by slowing down, keeping our attention focused and quiet, and seeing what offers itself into our thinking.

In this book, I offer my meditations on an exchange I shared with Tsuki, a five-year-old child. I often find myself speaking in metaphors in my conversations with children, using images and ideas to help us see beyond the immediate context and find unexpected perspectives. I use metaphors in my meditations in this book, too.

It's my instinct to look at things symbolically.

My mother talks in a way that recognizes a spirit in everything. She sees that everything is connected, and I've learned that from her.

I grew up in Japan, and was immersed in symbolic thinking. For example, one of the writing systems in Japanese, Kanji, draws on Chinese characters; you'll see Kanji throughout this book. Kanji is symbolic and cultivates a way of seeing symbols, of thinking symbolically. For example, this is the Kanji character for heart: 心. You see that character again here, on the bottom of another word, *forget*: 忘. The character on top means "to lose something" or "to vanish." So when I look at 忘, it gives me another way of understanding what it means to forget: when you forget, something vanishes from your heart. Growing up with Kanji, in combination with Hiragana and Katakana, is one of the many influences on my way of thinking metaphorically.

From Kanji to haiku, from Japanese cultural symbols like cherry blossoms to passionate teachers who gave me eyes for seeing connections between things like mathematics and baseball, astronomy and music, I learned that everything is related to everything else. Metaphors are a way for me to explore the connections between things.

I believe that metaphors help us look at things from a wider perspective; they help us think beyond what we're experiencing in the moment and see connections beyond the immediate circumstance. Metaphors offer a bigger lens, and help us make sense of what's happening by making connections to what else exists in the world.

And metaphors help us see many layers of meaning in children's play. In this book, I share the story of Tsuki's block play. On the surface, her play could be seen as a demonstration of her well-developed construction skills and her social competence. But when I look at Tsuki's play through the lens of metaphor, the meaning expands and carries me to consider my cultural history, our community's legacy, and our school's collective values. When I look through the kaleidoscope of metaphor, I grow new understandings of what it means to be human.

I invite you to look through the kaleidoscope with me.

After each of my meditations, I offer several questions for you to consider for your contemplation. Please give yourself the gift of time to hold the questions before moving on to the next chapter.

We're so often in a hurry with our work, even in our efforts to further our learning; we can get caught up in trying to be efficient and speedy in our reading and study. But it's a big loss when we don't make time to slow down and pay attention to our thinking and contemplations; we stay on the surface, instead of exploring the depths of ideas and questions and possibilities. When we slow down for ourselves, it gives us practice for slowing down with the children. When we are present in the moment for ourselves, it helps us be present in the moment with children.

My hope is that this book will provide an opportunity for you to pause and pay attention to your thinking and your wonderings, and to enjoy new and unexpected connections. This is an act of respect for yourself and for your work. It is a way to appreciate yourself. I encourage you to find a way to slow down enough to hold and ponder the questions. In the open space between the chapters, when you encounter my questions for contemplation, you may want to write, or sketch, or step outside to look at the sky, or make a cup of tea and sit in quiet. I invite you to join me in meditating on learning and growing with children.

# 1

Tsuki builds a motorcycle

Tsuki loves to build. She uses the large hollow blocks outside every single day. Her play reveals something about human nature that I find fascinating: building worlds that do not yet exist, making things that represent our reality, playing with ideas and crafting scenarios that come straight out of her imagination.

Tsuki starts her construction with a design in her mind, and knows which exact pieces she needs and specifically how to position them. She has a passion for building vehicles, including motorcycles; her dad rides a motorcycle, and her building is a connection to him. One particular day, Tsuki's block play began with her skillfully building a compact, handy motorcycle.

As she finished her building, Kouhei and Charlie came over to check out her motorcycle. Tsuki welcomed their arrival with a question: "Do you want to ride with me?" Kouhei and Charlie were certainly happy to hop on to the motorcycle, and squeezed themselves behind Tsuki.

Soon Fumiya, the twin brother of Kouhei, showed up. Seeing his brother having a blast on the motorcycle made Fumiya want to ride, too! But there seemed to be room only for two riders.

Fumiya kept his head down while showing his saddest look. Charlie got off the motorcycle, unsure about what to do. He wanted to get back on the same spot, right behind Kouhei, but recognized that, if he did, Fumiya couldn't have a turn. A silent moment for all of them.

"All right, guys." Tsuki looked at them and got off the driver seat. "I know what we can do." She began to collect and bring over more blocks. Tsuki, the engineer, began to expand her motorcycle with elbow grease. Her expression was intense and she worked hard. It appeared to my eye that Tsuki thought that she had a mission to accomplish: making an accommodation for her friends.

In the process of Tsuki's expansion of the motorcycle, Sebastian and Joseph, who had been around the area, got curious and excited. While Tsuki wanted them to wait to get on until the motorcycle was completely ready, they could not resist and kept attempting to do a test drive. Tsuki had to tell them several times, sternly, "Not yet, guys!" She was determined to finish the expansion of the motorcycle before anyone began to use it.

Ta-da! The motorcycle that Tsuki had envisioned came true. "OK, now it's ready!" Tsuki looked satisfied. This remarkable motorcycle attracted the attention of other children and they started to invite themselves over—probably more than Tsuki had imagined when she began to build. Tsuki was willing to let those children enjoy her newly innovated, transformed motorcycle. It became open for the public.

## ADJUSTMENT AND ASTONISHMENT

This motorcycle building happened before COVID-19. When the pandemic began, our school closed, and we were apart for three-and-a-half months. When we re-opened our school, I was very excited to reunite with the children in person! I felt like we were on a voyage of something new, something we had never experienced before. I was curious about what the children would remember from before our long closure.

Tsuki's motorcycle play, for instance, was still on my mind. It had been a magical moment: there was an intensity to her play, and strong determination. Her work to expand her motorcycle on that long-ago day had launched Tsuki into building gigantic motorcycles, moving beyond their usual compact nature. After that first motorcycle, she began to build motorcycles big enough to fit four or five people. This was her invention, this new sort of motorcycle. It reflected a new perspective for Tsuki, as she made sure there was enough room for other children; it seemed to be a way that she had decided to be of service, creating something useful for other children. I was curious: did Tsuki remember this play?

How would she interpret this months-ago block-building that took place pre-Covid? What would her reflections be, about this play? I was eager in my anticipation to see her reactions and hear her thoughts. I invited Tsuki to sit down with me to look at pictures of the motorcycle construction work that I had printed out.

Tsuki's face lit up when she saw the pictures of her and her friends with the blocks months earlier. "Ahhh, let me see . . ." she said, as she looked deliberately into each picture and retold the story.

"This is Kouhei and Charlie. They are riding a motorcycle. Kouhei is on. Fumiya wants to ride, too, and Charlie is thinking if he can share. I had an idea! Maybe I put a block so I can sit on there and Fumiya can be a driver. I need to make (an) adjustment so it won't hurt our butt." She chuckled. "Look what happened! Joseph and Sebastian want to go on. So I made that part, too, so everyone can get on! Then more people wanted to come, so I arranged. I made a seat for everyone. They are so happy. I'm happy, too."

After she described this construction and play, I invited Tsuki to "Draw what it was like when you were building." I often use representational drawing as a tool for thinking, inviting children to draw their ideas. This opens us into symbolic thinking that adds to children's understanding, and to my own.

When I encouraged Tsuki to draw her experience with the motorcycle, I imagined that she would draw a picture of herself building the motorcycle, or maybe a picture of riding on the motorcycle with her friends.

But to my surprise, Tsuki did not draw any blocks or the motorcycle. Instead, Tsuki drew a picture of herself with a lightbulb over her head. She also drew some hearts. After writing her name, Tsuki asked how to write the word, "Think." I was in astonishment.

Here's how Tsuki described her drawing: "That's me having an idea. Idea to 'adjustment' because then a lot of people can ride on the motorcycle." I was curious to find out what the word "adjustment" meant to her, so I asked for clarification:

"What does 'adjustment' mean?" Tsuki responded, " 'Adjustment' means that maybe you can use your thinking power to make things better. You can make something out of your brain." She paused and continued on. "Like fixing things. Like when other people may want to play with my creation."

This experience stayed with me for a long time. It meant much more than Tsuki's intricate "building skills" or Tsuki "learning to share." As I've thought about Tsuki's construction and her drawing and her words, the story opened into many resonances, provocations and metaphors.

## MEDITATION AND CONTEMPLATION

When have you been wonderfully astonished by a child in a way that left you wanting to keep thinking about your experience in order to understand it better?

Tsuki builds a motorcycle

## MEDITATION AND CONTEMPLATION

How do you understand the idea that slowing down helps
you connect with a child's thinking?

Tsuki builds a motorcycle

# 2

MEDITATION

## Shoshin wasuru bekarazu

初心忘るべからず

Tsuki loves to build. She uses the large hollow blocks outside every single day. Her play reveals something about human nature that I find fascinating: building worlds that do not yet exist, making things that represent our reality, playing with ideas and crafting scenarios that come straight out of her imagination.

The large hollow wood outdoor blocks have become a central part of our program's culture. They arrived at our school the same time as Tsuki did, and she's used them nearly every day for three years. We take the blocks for granted now, but there was a time when this particular type of block was very new to our eyes.

As I reflected on Tsuki's construction of a motorcycle with a seat for everyone and her drawing of herself thinking, I was reminded of the Japanese proverb, "Shoshin wasuru bekarazu." This means, literally, "Never forget the beginner's spirit." The proverb has many layers of complexity. "Don't lose your original intention, what got you here in the first place," it says. "Don't lose your initial enthusiasm." It's about self-development and growth; no matter how much experience you have, there is no such thing as being done growing. The implication of this proverb is that, as we gain more and more experiences, we shall cultivate our beginner's humility, our *shoshin*.

I'm not thinking of Tsuki as holding a "beginner's mind." Instead, we adults are the ones who need to cultivate our beginner's mind.

Certainly, children are at the "beginning" stage of their lives, but are they really "beginners" when it comes to noticing their world and being insightful? As I see them, children are the "experts" in noticing. They are filled with curiosity, trying to understand things deeply. They see the world as possibility. They are natural scientists. Their questions are profound. They remind us of the deep meaning of things. They make constant inquiries about being human; they are on a quest to learn about the world. I don't want to say they have beginners' minds, but expert minds.

It's us adults who need to bring ourselves back to our beginner's minds, to see the joy and brilliance in children's play.

*Shoshin* enables *kizuki*, which means noticing, being aware in a way that leads me to new realizations. *Kizuki*—awareness—is the turning wheel of the growing mind. *Kizuki* happens when I slow down to listen to children, when I try to really see the children's world, to seek connections and to understand their perspectives.

When I reflect back on Tsuki's motorcycle construction, when she intensely transformed her motorcycle, I realize that I watched her with my *shoshin*. That *shoshin* enabled me to see her remarkable flexibility and leadership, as she pursued her mission to accommodate her friends by adding more seats. But when I met with her later, to remember that block play with her, I let my *shoshin* slip, and made assumptions about what she might draw. Tsuki called me back to *shoshin*, surprising me with her lightbulb of thought.

I felt humble. My expectations had been totally wrong. This was an awakening, my own realization—*kizuki*, indeed. Tsuki reminded me that I shouldn't make assumptions about children's thinking, but, instead, should be always ready for surprises. I felt dazzled by Tsuki's expression in her drawing, and that dazzlement brought me back to the heart of why I love this work so much. It speaks to my *shoshin*: the passion, the core and the reason why I am in this field. This is the joy in this work for me, these moments that give me goosebumps when I encounter the limitless minds of human beings.

When I was growing up in Japan, adults often told us to "stay humble." That was a way of saying "keep growing." This is an aspect of beginner's mind: when we get used to doing something, we may lose our enthusiasm, or our original intention or goals. But when we stay humble, we stay grounded, we commit to keep growing. We respect everybody and everything as teachers.

"Shoshin wasuru bekarazu:" "Never forget the beginner's humility." I've seen Tsuki build many structures with the large hollow blocks. I want to pay attention, not look away with an assumption that, because I've seen her play with these blocks many times, I know what she's doing. I am reminded that each time will offer me new understandings and insights, not just about Tsuki, but about myself, and about being human.

## MEDITATION AND CONTEMPLATION

A beginner's mind helps us pay attention in ways that lead to new realizations. What helps you pay attention instead of making assumptions—or, when you do make assumptions, what helps you adjust your assumptions?

Shoshin wasuru bekarazu

## MEDITATION AND CONTEMPLATION

How do you experience the meaning of humility in your days with children?

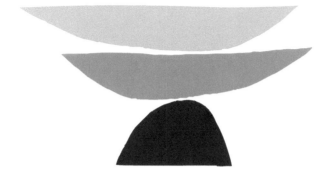

# 3

MEDITATION

Mitsugo no tamashii hyaku made

三つ子の魂百まで

"All right, guys." Tsuki looked at them and got off the driver seat. "I know what we can do." She began to collect and bring over more blocks. Tsuki, the engineer, began to expand her motorcycle with elbow grease. Her expression was intense and she worked hard. It appeared to my eye that Tsuki thought that she had a mission to accomplish: making an accommodation for her friends.

In the process of Tsuki's expansion of the motorcycle, Sebastian and Joseph, who had been around the area, got curious and excited. While Tsuki wanted them to wait to get on until the motorcycle was completely ready, they could not resist and kept attempting to do a test drive. Tsuki had to tell them several times, sternly, "Not yet, guys!" She was determined to finish the expansion of the motorcycle before anyone began to use it.

Ta-da! The motorcycle that Tsuki had envisioned came true. "OK, now it's ready!" Tsuki looked satisfied. This remarkable motorcycle attracted the attention of other children and they started to invite themselves over—probably more than Tsuki had imagined when she began to build. Tsuki was willing to let those children enjoy her newly innovated, transformed motorcycle. It became open for the public.

When I watch Tsuki in the spirit of *kizuki*, with awareness and an openness to new recognitions, my understanding of who Tsuki is continues to deepen. Tsuki is a builder, a creative thinker, welcoming of her friends, quick to make adjustments to make things better for everyone, proud of her inventiveness and appreciative of the provocation by her friends to expand her thinking; she's growing into being a leader.

This person that Tsuki is now is the person she'll carry forward through her life ahead. That's what the Japanese proverb, "Mitsugo no tamashii hyaku made," teaches us: "The soul of the three-year-old child is the soul of that person at a hundred years old." And our mission as educators is to see, respect, and nurture the uniqueness of each child.

Being fully present to each child, in the here and now, is the most powerful thing we can do to help the children learn to deeply know themselves. This is our great responsibility.

Sometimes childhood is viewed as a time of preparation for "real" life: for school and for the roles of adulthood. But children are living their real life: they are experiencing life itself! We are working with children who are here with us now, and that's who we should be honoring. It is important to see and hear who each child is now: that soul—the light within, their life essence, the whole of who they are—will stay with them through their lives. We must nourish the young souls that will be carried into their older years.

When I think of Tsuki—her determination, her strong mindset, her curiosity and openness—I see that her character has continuity. I've known Tsuki since she was two, when she joined our program, and I've enjoyed these traits shining through her over the years. I like this phrase, *limitless mind*: it describes Tsuki. She believes anything is possible: her mind is boundless, and she is fearless.

When I am fully present to Tsuki, I'm attending to that unique essence of who she is. I want to preserve that and help it blossom, not try to change it or to graft something different onto it. It is our responsibility to adjust our thinking, to accommodate who a child is and respond to that person's soul, to shine a light on who they are. It is *kizuki*—noticing, being aware—that helps me see each child.

I believe this is one of children's human rights: the right to be seen. The right to be who they are, fully living their lives. To be nurtured as who they are now, because that soul is their soul through their lives: *Mitsugo no tamashii hyaku made*.

When we enact this human right for children, we enrich our own souls, too. It lifts us out of the confined roles of educators, and asks us to see another person from the perspective of a fellow human being. We encounter the many colorful ways that people can be, rather than relating to children through a narrow lens of "learning goals" or "school readiness." And this nurtures our growth, too. When we are present, human to human, we can let our souls be seen, too.

There's another Japanese saying that challenges me to stay present to each moment with a child: "Ichigo ichie," which reminds us that we have just this "one time." Consider every encounter as the only encounter, as once in a lifetime: 一期一会. I want to see children through the lens of joy, honoring the souls that each of them will carry with them through their lives.

## MEDITATION AND CONTEMPLATION

How has your soul—your light, your essential self—been nurtured through your life?

.

.

## MEDITATION AND CONTEMPLATION

What helps you see the soul of each child, the soul that they will carry until they are a hundred years old?

Mitsugo no tamashii hyaku made

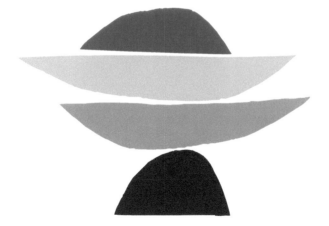

# 4

MEDITATION

## Core values to support shoshin

I invited Tsuki to "Draw what it was like when you were building." I imagined that she would draw a picture of herself building the motorcycle, or maybe a picture of riding on the motorcycle with her friends.

But to my surprise, Tsuki did not draw any blocks or the motorcycle. Instead, Tsuki drew a picture of herself with a lightbulb on her head. She also drew some hearts. After writing her name, Tsuki asked how to write the word, "Think." I was in astonishment.

Here's how Tsuki described her drawing: "That's me having an idea. Idea to 'adjustment' because then a lot of people can ride on the motorcycle." I was curious to find out what the word "adjustment" meant to her, so I asked for clarification: "What does 'adjustment' mean?" Tsuki responded, "'Adjustment' means that maybe you can use your thinking power to make things better. You can make something out of your brain." She paused and continued on. "Like fixing things. Like when other people may want to play with my creation."

With her drawing and her description, Tsuki shook me out of my assumptions. I thought she would draw herself working on the motorcycle, or the children riding on it, but instead, she showed me herself thinking. This was humbling, and an awakening for me about the pre-conceptions I held about what she was going to offer. Why did I already have a pre-image of what she was going to do? Tsuki called me back to my beginner's humility.

One thing that calls me into *shoshin* is the statement of core values in our program. Those values serve as lenses that allow me to see a child's play from a range of perspectives and exploring a range of meanings. Our program's values nourish *shoshin* and *shoshin* enables us to see these values in action.

After my awakening about the unconscious assumptions I had held about Tsuki's story, I turned to our school core values to see more deeply into Tsuki's offering.

## OUR CORE VALUES

Several years ago, in an effort to align our practice with our aspirations, our staff worked to name and make visible the values at the heart of our program. We wanted to honor the Japanese culture that connects our school community and that is our inheritance, and also to call forward the culture we want to create. During this process, we committed to actively construct the meaning of the values we named, and not be satisfied with just the words. These values would become the lenses through which we would examine our practice and see the children.

We called these "core values in the Japanese cultural context," values that spoke to us as Japanese people and that reflected how we grew up in Japan. The specific terms are Japanese words; these were the starting place for us to talk about their meanings and to develop shared understandings. We paid attention to the nuances of the words: not just the literal translations, but their resonance and meaning for how to live in the world.

Here are our core values:

**Omoiyari** 思いやり:

*This is a way of treating all beings: offering kindness, compassion and love, being thoughtful and mindful, respecting others and embracing diversity.*

**Nintai** 忍耐:

*This speaks of perseverance and endurance, coping with challenges, being patient and resilient.*

**Kansha** 感謝:

*This value is about being grateful. It keeps us connected to the joy of feeling appreciated and appreciative, living with gratitude.*

**Souzousei** 創造性:

*This is the creativity of an innovator, a pioneer, a problem solver, an inventor.*

**Gakumon** 学問:

*This refers to deep learning, to taking an inquiry journey, to never-ending learning, being a critical thinker, having an inquisitive mind, seeking multiple perspectives.*

## CORE VALUES AS A LENS

Our core values support me in an inquiry process that helps me understand children—and all of us human beings—more deeply. When I look at a child's play through the lens of our core values, I get to know that child's soul with more nuance and complexity. And when I see the values brought to life in children's play, my understanding of the meaning of the values becomes more nuanced, too.

This happened in my exchange with Tsuki. "*How are our core values expressed in Tsuki's story?*" I asked myself. My reflections on this question helped me see Tsuki more fully, and also helped me understand the values better.

Tsuki demonstrated *omoiyari* when she was building, with her inventive thinking about how she could include others in her motorcycle. And in her drawing and her description of making an adjustment to make things better, Tsuki illuminated the spirit of *omoiyari*, its feel of warmth and compassion. She knew she was being a kind friend, and felt happy about that.

Making a seat for everyone: that is *omoiyari*. And it demonstrates *nintai*, too. When she was working with the blocks, Tsuki was quite tolerant of Sebastian and Joseph when they inserted themselves into her work. And she persevered to figure out how to complete what she'd envisioned, drawing on *nintai.* "All right, guys, I know what we can do," she said, and got to work carrying out her plan.

Tsuki's *kansha* was pure and joyful. "I had an idea!" she exclaimed to me, remembering the block play. "Look what happened! I made a seat for everyone. They are so happy. I'm happy, too." She appreciated her accomplishment—both the actual construction and her work to accommodate other children's desire to ride the motorcycle. She was grateful for the process and for the circle of friends around her. As I listened to her describe her thinking, I thought how happy she looked, like something genuine was coming from her heart: a sense of joy, of satisfaction, of pleasure that she had impacted people so positively. She was happy that she had made others happy: that is emotional intelligence, for sure!

Certainly, Tsuki showed *souzousei* when she constructed the motorcycle, by making an "adjustment" and using "thinking power to make things better." And, later, drawing herself thinking demonstrated *souzousei*: her drawing was itself a creative act, as she represented "thinking power" with a light bulb and "making things better" with hearts. Such symbolic images!

Tsuki illustrated the nuances of *gakumon* when she engineered and re-engineered the motorcycle to expand it, to make a seat for everyone. And our reflection together was *gakumon* for both of us, deep learning, together. The story of Tsuki's motorcycle came alive for me when we sat together to talk and draw; I learned about how Tsuki thinks about her block-building, and how she thinks about thinking.

And, now, writing this, I realize that my process of reflecting and writing is *gakumon* for **me**. I've been focusing on Tsuki and how she inhabits the core values, and I haven't been thinking about applying those values to my own action and reflection. I discovered a missing piece in my thinking! I want to bring *kizuki*—my awareness and attention—to how the central essences of these five values are part of my reflections about my experience with Tsuki. How do I live these values, myself? This is a question for me to ponder. This is gakumon for me.

## MEDITATION AND CONTEMPLATION

How might you describe a core value that's at the heart of your life with children?

How does that value influence how you see Tsuki?

Core values to support shoshin

77

## MEDITATION AND CONTEMPLATION

How could you keep nurturing this value in yourself, so that it is visible and tangible, and an intentional part of your life and your days with children?

# 5

MEDITATION

## Ma te tiro tomuri, ka kitea tomua

"Look what happened! Joseph and Sebastian want to go on. So I made that part, too, so everyone can get on! Then more people wanted to come, so I arranged. I made a seat for everyone. They are so happy. I'm happy, too."

……

Tsuki drew a picture of herself with a lightbulb on her head. She also drew some hearts. … "That's me having an idea. Idea to 'adjustment' because then a lot of people can ride on the motorcycle. 'Adjustment' means that maybe you can use your thinking power to make things better."

*A seat for everyone. Make adjustments, use your thinking power to make things better for people. Tsuki's words sounded like a metaphor to me, not just instruction for how to build a bigger motorcycle, but for how to live in the world. We have to live for what's right, act for justice, become strong advocates for democracy: that's the metaphor I heard in Tsuki's reflections.*

## CONSIDERING OUR LEGACY, PAST, PRESENT, AND FUTURE

I had the good fortune to participate in an early childhood education study tour to New Zealand several years ago. One of the provocations that had the biggest impact for me came from Heather Durham, the director of Helensville Montessori; she said, "If you want to do Reggio, you're in the wrong place. If you want to do Montessori, you're in the wrong era. We all need to find our path to move forward." Later, in some follow-up reading after my study tour, I encountered this Maori saying: *Ma te tiro tomuri, ka kitea tomua*: Reflect on the past to guide the future[1].

This was a wake-up call for me, and really resonated. I work at a Japanese-English bilingual, multicultural preschool. I asked myself, "What is our identity? We have inherited powerful roots as a school; what are the deep meanings of those cultural roots?" These questions led me to educate myself about our school community's history, so that I better understood the legacy we had been given. And I discovered a legacy of social justice activism.

---

1) Trish Thomas and Sara Pillay, "Mindful of our Past, Optimistic for our Future," Exchange, March/April (2014)

The first generation of women to immigrate to San Francisco from Japan—*Issei* women—led a campaign to build the Japanese YWCA in 1932; that's the building that our school is in, in Japantown in San Francisco. The *Issei* women were determined to create their own YWCA because they couldn't join any other branch: those were racially segregated and didn't allow Japanese members. They couldn't even hold the title to the property for their Y outright, but had to lease it, because the Alien Land Law prohibited immigrant people from owning land.

They recruited Julia Morgan as the architect for their project. Julia Morgan, a white woman, had graduated from U.C. Berkeley in 1894 as the first female to earn a degree in civil engineering. She donated her efforts on the Japanese YWCA, working pro bono for the *Issei* women, who were her sisters in defying the social order of the time, not conforming to the traditional roles that relegated women to second class citizens.

This history moves me. To the Issei women, I say: thank you for being pioneers and for your *nintai* (resiliency) and strength. After so much effort to build your beautiful building, you were incarcerated, forced to move into camps far from your homes, robbed of the joy you could have had under this roof.

To Julia Morgan, I say: thank you for partnering with a marginalized community, for fighting for your own education and using your privilege to stand with those who had less power than you. To all of you, I say: We will carry on your message of hope, resiliency and *omoiyari* (compassion), and continue to stand for what is right. Your legacy has helped us grow into a strong community.

It is in this spirit of honoring our legacy that Tsuki's words become a metaphor: *Build a seat for everyone. Make adjustments, use your thinking power to make things better for people.* Tsuki reminds us of the mentality we need to bring to the world. It is the same mentality that the Issei women and Julia Morgan left for us—resilience and fortitude, determination to fight injustice and to work to make the world a more welcoming, fair place. This is what the world needs, to fuel the movement for racial justice and to build bridges across the many divides in our society. When I listened to Tsuki's words, in the societal context of repeated and ongoing acts of injustice, I thought, "A five-year-old is saying such powerful things. What are we grown-ups doing? This is how we all should think!"

We in early childhood education are with children at the beginning of their lives: they are young, but behind them are many layers of history. And ahead of them, we want to create a world of justice and democracy. We all have a shared responsibility as ancestors, building the dispositions and skills to create a more just world. It is the capacity for active, rigorous thinking (Tsuki's light bulb!) bound together with compassion (the heart in Tsuki's drawing) that inspire us to make a seat for everyone, and to use our power to make changes for the better.

*Ma te tiro tomuri, ka kitea tomua*: Reflect on the past to move forward. Remember where you come from, so you can get where you are going. I think of the legacy we inherit and the legacy we create. When Julia Morgan and the Issei women made seats for Japanese families in a society that devalued them, they were building towards a more just world. This is the inheritance that we are stewarding for the future. It's an invitation for all of us, not just us at our school; we all have histories and stories that we can draw on to help us move forward. We can all be co-conspirators for justice.

Ma te tiro tomuri, ka kitea tomua

## MEDITATION AND CONTEMPLATION

What story or history that has shaped your identity do you want to call forward in your work?

Ma te tiro tomuri, ka kitea tomua

## MEDITATION AND CONTEMPLATION

What story are you creating today that will be
a legacy for the future?

# 6

MEDITATION

Jyuunin toiro

十人十色

"I made a seat for everyone. They are so happy. I'm happy, too."

Tsuki's story is not more extraordinary than other children's stories. All children carry these rich stories with them. It is up to us to see and notice the stories that each child offers. The essence of that noticing is the power of *kizuki*: awareness, mindfulness, recognizing. It is in the moment we pause. It is in our willingness to see and to listen.

Our beginner's humility allows us to see with new eyes. As we continue to grow throughout our lives, we will always have opportunities to embrace a beginner's mind and to recommit to a *shoshin* mindset. Our values keep our gaze on how we want to live and what we want to call forward in children and in ourselves. Our heritage reminds us of the footprints we are choosing to leave for the generations after. From this grounding, we begin to see the complexity and richness of each moment of children's play—and the depths and magnificence of each child's personhood.

I think of the proverb *Jyuunin toiro*, ten people, ten colors, which calls attention to the diversity and uniqueness of each person: each individual is different. When you multiply and combine people, it's not just ten colors, it's so many colors that would be created—in an exponential way! Jyuunin toiro reminds us that every child has these rich stories and that, together, they create a beautiful tapestry. What a rich world we get to be in!

## MEDITATION AND CONTEMPLATION

Tsuki created a proverb: *Make adjustments, make a seat for everyone.*

How could you capture your intention for your days with children in the language of a proverb? What proverb would you create?

Jyuunin toiro

TSUKI THINK

# About Misa

Misa, a native of Japan, came to San Francisco Bay Area after high school to explore the wider world and to attend university. While majoring in Child and Adolescent Development with a focus on Young Child and Family, Misa had opportunities to work with diverse groups of preschoolers in different settings and found deep fascination with being in a classroom with young children side-by-side.

Misa has been at a Japanese bilingual preschool program, Nihonmachi Little Friends, for the last 17 years. Her great joy comes from being a co-researcher along with the children for inquisitive pursuits every day and having collaborative partnerships with other educators.

Misa finds it inspiring to participate in reflective learning community for dialogues with other professionals, from national to international, who are in various roles in the field, to envision what's possible as a greater wholeness.

Misa enjoys going on a hike, traveling anywhere near and far, and finds peace with engaging in creative arts and processes.

# Acknowledgments 感謝

Heartfelt thanks to Eliana Elias for bringing up this wild idea to me and believing that I can join the ROW collection as an author. I appreciate Yuji Uchida for being my sounding board throughout the writing journey and sharing his insights. Special thanks to Barb Yasui, Debbie LeeKeenan, Diane Rawlins, George Alonzo, Nicky Byers, and Pam Oken-Wright for making time to read the initial draft of this book and offer their thoughtful feedback. I am grateful to Cathy Inamasu for being a mother of our vibrant learning community.

I am fortunate to get to experience the richness of life together with all the children, families, and colleagues. My eternal gratitude to my family and friends for your love and support. To Ann, Margie and the incredible Exchange team, thank you for all the listening, your wisdom, creativity, and making my story come alive.

Love and gratitude to you, Tsuki. Thank you for sharing what it means to live your life fully.

心からありがとう。

## From Reading to Thinking: A Protocol for Reflection and Learning

Like you—like every educator—Misa works in a program where many things compete for her attention. The beacon that helps her navigate these demands is her decision to hold herself accountable to each child's human right to be seen. This fundamental commitment illuminates her way forward, and allows her to see the children "through the lens of joy, honoring the souls that each of them will carry with them through their lives."

Misa uses her values, her cultural touchstones, the history and context of her school to help her focus her attention on the children, seeking the many meanings in their play. She draws on the legacy of the Issei women and their partner, Julia Morgan, who committed their attention to the human rights of the Japanese American community in San Francisco to create new possibilities for themselves and for future generations. Misa's meditations demonstrate the power of attention to "lift us out of the confined roles of educators" in order to see the children "from the perspective of a fellow human being."

As you read Misa's meditations, what stirred in you that lifted you out of the confined role of an educator? Perhaps, as you read, you became aware of your beliefs about what children deserve, and about what you want to hold yourself accountable to—as an educator and as a human being. You may have felt yourself making adjustments to your thinking as you bumped up against internal resistance or hesitations that Misa's meditations sparked in you. Perhaps you found your way to your own metaphors or proverbs that illuminate the meaning of your work or that help you see yourself in a new way. To sustain the thinking and wondering that you've done as you've read, you may decide to revisit the questions for contemplation at the end of each chapter, allowing them to reverberate in new ways.

One of the questions that Misa asks us to contemplate is: *What helps you see the soul of each child?* This question—and, indeed, Misa's whole book—assumes that you dearly desire to see, and to honor and nurture, each child's full human self. Misa writes:

> When I am fully present to Tsuki, I'm attending to that unique essence of who she is. I want to preserve that and help it blossom, not try to change it or to graft something different onto it. It is our responsibility to adjust our thinking, to accommodate who a child is and respond to that person's soul, to shine a light on who they are. It is kizuki—noticing, being aware—that helps me see each child.

*I believe this is one of children's human rights: the right to be seen. The right to be who they are, fully living their lives. To be nurtured as who they are now.*

We hope that you share, with Misa, this deep-held intention to be fully present to each child, by noticing, being aware, adjusting your thinking, responding to each child's soul. By paying attention. We hope that, like Misa, you are committed to resisting the narrow definitions of what it means to be an educator, by shifting your role from teaching to thinking and wondering about who each child is so that you can "respond to that person's soul."

The Thinking Lens protocol (fully described in *From Teaching to Thinking: A Pedagogy for Reimagining Our Work*) offers a practice to strengthen our capacity for paying attention to each child, and for nurturing each child's full-souled engagement with life and its wonderments. The Thinking Lens slows us down and asks us to savor and to contemplate the nuances of moments we share with children, rather than seizing those moments as opportunities to leap in with a teaching goal or with an assessment checklist. The Thinking Lens invites us to articulate our values, notice and disrupt our assumptions, and consider a range of perspectives in order to add complexity to our thinking.

In these ways, the Thinking Lens reminds us, in Misa's words, "that each time will offer me new understandings and insights, not just about [a child], but about myself, and about being human." The Thinking Lens is a tool for developing *kizuki*—"noticing, being aware in a way that leads us to new realizations"—and for cultivating *shoshin*, the humility and curiosity of the beginner's mind.

As you read this book, you encountered Misa's invitations to pause for contemplation and meditation. Now, we invite you to add to those contemplations by revisiting the book's ideas in the context of the guideposts in the Thinking Lens. We offer these questions to support your study and to help you articulate your learning, perhaps in writing, and then in conversation with colleagues and pedagogical companions.

**Know yourself. Open your heart to this moment.**
What touched you about this story?

Recall a time when you slowed down to listen deeply to a child. How would you describe the impact of that experience on you? On the child? On your relationship?

How do the values that Misa writes about connect with values that you hold for your teaching practice?

How does the idea of "teaching as a meditation" resonate with you?

**Take the children's points of view.**

Misa reminds us that educators do well to keep a "beginner's mind" to ward off assumptions about what children may do, say, or mean in their actions. Can you recall an experience that helps you understand the value of keeping a "beginner's mind" as you seek to understand a child's perspective?

How does Tsuki's drawing of herself thinking and making adjustments provoke your assumptions about the capabilities of young children?

---

**Examine the environment.**

What aspects of the physical and social environment at Misa's school supported Tsuki to think and make adjustments?

Misa's school holds five values at the heart of their community. How do those values create an environment for educators that supports their reflection and learning?

---

**Collaborate with others to expand perspectives.**

Misa's inner dialogue involves a collaboration with cultural values and an engagement with the legacy of her school's building. What values and legacies might you call forward to expand your thinking?

Are there proverbs or aspects of cultural wisdom that you and colleagues could bring to a discussion of how this book has helped you make adjustments in your thinking?

_____

**Reflect and take action.**
Building on your reflections, write a statement that describes the learning that you will carry with you from _Making Adjustments_.

What will you do differently in your work, because of reading this book?

_____

Reading a book is an investment of time and attention. To make the most of that investment, revisit sections of the book that engaged or confused you. Find study companions to help you reflect on the meditations in _Making Adjustments_. Commit yourself to transform your reading from a passive experience of listening to a good story to an active engagement with thinking and questioning. Reading a book in this way becomes professional development.

May you, like Misa, encounter many moments with children that give you goosebumps, as you "encounter the limitless minds of human beings." And may you, like Misa, "see children through the lens of joy, honoring the souls that each of them will carry with them through their lives."

**—*Ann Pelo* and *Margie Carter***
  Editors of the *Reimagining Our Work* (ROW) Collection

  Authors of *From Teaching to Thinking: A Pedagogy for Reimagining Our Work*